Zodiac Gift Guide

Gift Ideas for Sun Signs

Carol Sandy

ACS Publications

Zodiac Gift Guide
Third Edition

© copyright 2007, 2009, 2010 by Carol Sandy

First Edition, first printing: 2007, AstroWindows
Second Edition, first printing 2009, ACS Publications
Third Edition, first printing 2010, ACS Publications

Cover, book design and zodiac circle art
by Maria Kay Simms

Other illustrations from
Art Explosion licensed clip art
from Nova Development
© 1995-2001

International Standard Book Number: 978-1-934976-15-9

Published by ACS Publications
an imprint of Starcrafts LLC
334-A Calef Hwy., Epping, NH 03042
http://www.acspublications.com
http://www.starcraftspublishing.com
http://www.astrocom.com

Printed in the United States of America

The **Zodiac Gift Guide**
provides you with
twelve personality portraits,
one for each sign of the zodiac.
It is hoped that these images
and gift suggestions will inspire
you to consider astrology
and also use your own
imagination and creativity
in your future gift selections.

Contents

♈ ♉ ♊ ♋ ♌ ♍ ♎ ♏ ♐ ♑ ♒ ♓

Introduction

Selecting a gift for another person should be an enjoyable experience; however, because of the uncertainty over "how well" the gift will be received, this activity is frequently filled with anxiety and frustration. Knowing something about an individual's personality can be very beneficial in this regard.

The celestial science of astrology provides us with useful information about an individual's nature, temperament, needs, desires, tastes and focus in life.

In ancient times, it was observed, that those born around the same time of the year shared similar traits. These similarities were grouped into four categories or natural elements; each element being reflective of a particular life experience. The four elements, fire, earth, air and water were further divided into twelve zodiac signs; in order to indicate specific attitudes, behaviors and characteristics. The fire signs, Aries, Leo and Sagittarius experience life on the energy plane, being physical, energetic and self expressive. The earth signs, Taurus, Virgo and Capricorn, experience life on the material plane, being involved with the practical concerns of daily living. The air signs, Gemini, Libra and Aquarius experience life on the mental plane, sharing thoughts, ideas and concepts. Last, the water signs, Cancer, Scorpio and Pisces experience life on the emotional plane, being highly attuned to their intuition, feelings and psychic powers.

In astrology, the most significant energy pattern of an individual is his zodiac sun sign, which is based upon his date, time and place of birth. However, it is important to note, that an individual is much more than just his sun sign, but a combination of many different energy patterns. Also, those having the same zodiac sun sign are similar, but uniquely different from one another. The sun sign represents the core, the "very essence" of an individual: the physical vitality, will, ego, self expression, life experiences, needs, desires, life lessons, the qualities the individual wants to cultivate, and most importantly, his life's direction and purpose.

The **Zodiac Gift Guide** offers the reader two avenues in which to select a gift; choose a gift according to an individual's zodiac sun sign alone, or choose a gift according to the characteristics of a particular element or zodiac sign.

Increase Your Selections

In general, individuals enjoy being around their natural element, literally; the fire signs, Aries, Leo and Sagittarius, like cookouts, campfires and being outdoors. The earth signs, Taurus, Virgo and Capricorn, take pleasure in working with the soil, building sand castles and climbing up mountains. The air signs, Gemini, Libra and Aquarius, although they spend most of their time indoors, do enjoy air travel and engaging in wind sports. The water signs, Cancer, Scorpio and Pisces, all take delight in being around bodies of water.

Having an understanding of the inner dynamics of the twelve zodiac signs can increase your gift selections; for example, zodiac signs sharing the same element will have similar interests and tastes. Also, each of the twelve zodiac signs has their own polarity or opposite sign. The six individual pairs focus on similar issues; however, each sign has a different perspective. The two opposite signs, in conjunction with one another, present a balanced point of view.

In an attempt to create a state of equilibrium within oneself, the individual on a subconscious level, frequently takes on the characteristics of his sun sign polarity, or becomes attracted to those individuals who have the qualities of his opposite sun sign.

If you need more gift suggestions; look to the opposite sign for additional ideas.

Opposite Signs

Aries	Libra
Taurus	Scorpio
Gemini	Sagittarius
Cancer	Capricorn
Leo	Aquarius
Virgo	Pisces

ARIES
March 20/21 - April 19

has the Consciousness of a "Knight in Shining Armor"

Aries is a sign that is primarily focused on: the individual self, personal initiative and self actualization, action, challenges and confrontation, work, weapons, the military and fire, metal, machinery and hardware.

The sign Aries represents the "pioneer", the enterprising individual, who always takes the lead, and who is always on the "cutting edge". This highly energetic, enthusiastic fire sign thrives on excitement and competition, likes fun activities, enjoys building things, takes delight in playing practical jokes, wears tailored clothes and looks "good" in a uniform, favors the color red, and is fond of: hats, boots and leather, also motor vehicles, especially trucks, motorcycles and heavy machinery.

Aries is the first sign of the zodiac; thus symbolizing "new beginnings and new ventures."

When selecting a gift for an "Aries type" person, think in terms of the "newest and latest".

Fearless • Fiery • Forceful

Gift Suggestions for

Aries

Purchase items that are monogrammed, personalized or have the number "1" prominently displayed. Give things associated with physical activity, such as: a membership to a fitness club, classes for kick boxing or martial arts, sessions with a personal trainer and exercise or sports equipment.

Surprise the Aries by turning his basement into a well-equipped workshop or home gym. Purchase items associated with the face, head or hair: a pair of "sharp looking" earrings, "state of the art" grooming aids, teeth or facial treatments and a gift card to a hair salon or spa.

Choose items, books or magazine subscriptions pertaining to: self-improvement, body building, adventure and travel, sports, firearms, and entrepreneurship, also Hot Rods, trains and model railroading.

Look in, or give: a gift card to the computer or electronics stores, the military surplus and the auto, tattoo and clothing shops. Select things associated with the Aries work: a tool case or kit, personalized stationary and a high-tech cell phone.

The Aries is known for being "fast paced", give: a speed boat, power tools, a food processor, a hot beverage system, a microwave or high speed Internet service. Consider giving: a horse, a dirt bike, a little red sports car, western apparel and a statue of an armored knight, also video war games, a fire pit, a cutlery set, a barbecue grill, a personal horoscope reading or a trip to a paint ball camp.

Give things that will "fire up" the spirit; such as tickets to: the rodeo, the auto races and the demolition derby, a boxing match, a hockey game or a rock concert.

THE Aries

Wants to be First

TAURUS
April 19 - May 20

has the Consciousness of a "Builder"

Taurus is the second sign of the zodiac, and is primarily focused on: affection, personal resources and finances (how to earn, save and spend money), material possessions, *values,* self -worth, beautification, earthly pleasures and artistic expression. The sign Taurus represents the *"business person"*; the *security conscious* individual, who requires a *return* for his time, effort or investment. This *stable*, even-tempered earth sign takes *pleasure* in his home, garden and personal *comforts*, is fond of "good food", especially sweets, enjoys shopping and socializing, favors the pastel colors, and has an appreciation for: pleasant surroundings, attractive clothing, jewelry and accessories.

When you are selecting a gift for a "Taurus type" person, choose things of "quality," and that are practical, tasteful or sensual.

Purposeful • Productive Patient

Gift Suggestions for

TAURUS

Give items that will "excite the senses: colognes, colorful balloons and scented candles, beauty treatments, a foot or shower massager, fragrant flowers, a day at a spa and music CD's, also tickets to a concert or a Broadway show.

Look for things that are soft and silky: a cashmere sweater, a plush robe, a silk scarf or tie, Egyptian cotton sheets or a cuddly toy animal. Consider gastronomical delights: a dinner at a "five star" restaurant, gourmet meats and cheeses, a box of candy, a basket of fruit and a luscious three layer cake.

Visit the garden center, housewares and appliance departments for items that are useful and "eye pleasing": garden tools, an adorable bird house, a cookie jar, a throw blanket, a big screen TV and a music sound system. Purchase items that are associated with *physical* comforts: A pair of comfy slippers, a hammock, a reclining chair, a goose-down comforter, a hot tub and a motor vehicle. Give items, books or subscriptions related to: beauty, fashion, arts and crafts, interior decorating, baking, consumer info, business and financial planning. Purchase items related to work: a handsome briefcase, a stylish desk set, office furniture and a gift card to the computer, electronics or stationery stores. Consider things that will aid the individual in his artistic pursuits: art supplies, classes for singing, dancing, or painting, also cake decorating, floral arranging and ceramics. Select items associated with money: a wallet or hand bag, a LARGE piggy bank, a gift card to a shopping mall, a money tree and board games that use "play money", also don't forget the "cash;" it always brings a smile.

THE Taurus
has a Need to Acquire

GEMINI
May 21 - June 20

has the Consciousness of a "Student"

Gemini is the third sign of the zodiac, and is primarily focused on: the cognitive processes, verbal and written communications, short distance travel, transportation, agreements and contracts, current events, education, siblings, the local community and neighbors.

The sign Gemini represents the "journalist"; the curious individual, who collects and disseminates information. This logical, loquacious air sign enjoys mental sport and debate, also reading, socializing and exchanging tidbits of information, takes an interest in the news, the weather and the latest trends, has a good sense of humor, makes purchases in quantities of two's, likes variety, trivia and clever gadgets, is receptive to all colors, and is particularly fond of stripes.

When you are selecting a gift for a "Gemini type" person, choose things that will promote or facilitate travel, mobility, learning and communications.

Agile • Alert • Articulate

Gift Suggestions for
GEMINI

Give: books, magazine subscriptions or DVD's that are topical or popular, also a membership to a book club, educational courses and CD's, puzzles and games, especially word games.

Consider giving: a mobile or messaging phone, a mail box, walkie-talkies, a lap top computer, a printer and a fax machine; also look in the stationery store for a fountain pen, an address book, a briefcase and a personal diary or journal. The hands play an important role in the Gemini's life; think about giving: a gift card for a hand or nail treatment, a ring, a manicure set, and a pair of soft flexible gloves. Also, consider games or hobbies in which the hands are highlighted; such as: a deck of playing cards, a chess set, a needle point kit and a set of golf clubs. Think about turning the Gemini's spare room into a study; shop for a desk set, a pair of "interesting looking" bookends, a reading lamp and a comfortable chair. Consider: a motor vehicle, auto accessories and a gasoline gift card, also a membership to an auto club, a GPS and a set of lightweight luggage. Purchase: walking shoes, a pedometer, skates or a bicycle. Give: computer software, a course in writing or speaking, personalized address labels, a letter opener, a horoscope reading, a *Farmer's Almanac* and a newspaper from the Gemini's birth date; also look at a joke or cartoon book, a TV, a radio (all types) and a home weather station. Think about tickets for: a sporting or social event, a scenic bus or train ride, a car show or a museum exhibit; also consider a night out at a comedy club or a dinner at a restaurant that offers a buffet.

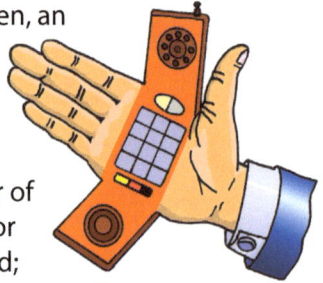

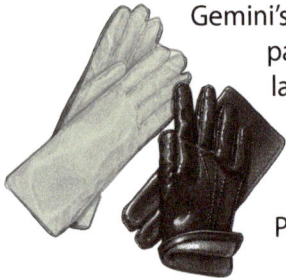

THE Gemini
Needs Mental Stimulation

CANCER
June 21 - July 22

has the Consciousness of a "Nester/Homebody"

Cancer is the fourth sign of the zodiac, and is primarily focused on: "the necessities of life", the mother, the home and the family, women, infants and the public, also approval, emotional needs, the subconscious, early childhood conditioning, memories, food and all types of liquids.

The sign Cancer represents the "nurturer", the maternal individual, who uses his instincts to care after others. This traditional, very private water sign remembers the "little things" in life, enjoys celebrating the holidays with the family, loves dairy products, Norman Rockwell prints and the aroma of "fresh bread", takes delight in gardening, is an avid collector, believes in having a "nest egg", favors the colors blue and silver, and has a fondness for: fireplaces, rocking chairs, family photos, memorabilia, classic cars and movies.

When you are selecting a gift for a "Cancer type" person, choose items that are thoughtful, sentimental, or related to the domestic scene.

Sensitive • Sympathetic
Sincere

Gift Suggestions for
CANCER

Give: beach, boating and water sports paraphernalia, especially look at the fishing and snorkeling gear. Consider: a seafood dinner, a fish aquarium, a hot tub, a cruise to an island and tickets to a Water Park, boat or Ice Show.

Purchase items, books or subscriptions about: financial planning, women topics, the family, cooking, antiques, lighthouses and home projects. Visit: the music, religious and photography stores, the garden center, the crafts shop and the housewares department; also check-out the country stores and catalogs.

Give things that will bring the family together: board games, tickets to the circus and dinner at a "home-style" restaurant.

Consider: a family size picnic basket or a barbecue grill, also a swimming pool, a big screen TV and a family portrait. Shop for items that will make the office or home "look and *feel*" cozy and comfy: ceramic nick knacks, lace doilies and picture frames, also table linens, holiday decorations, a house plant, an embroidered pillow, a decorative doormat and a hand-made quilt.

Consider: a charm bracelet, pearl jewelry, a sentimental keepsake, a *family* heirloom, a music box, a snow globe and a doll house, also a "ship in a bottle", a jute box, a coupon organizer, a wallet, a purse, a coin collection or bank, square dance lessons, tickets to a musical or country fair, a fruit basket and a "home cooked" meal. Browse through the culinary shop; especially look at the coffee grinders, the pasta, bread and ice cream makers.

Think about: trips to a winery, an historical seaport or a religious site, also consider a weekend stay at a "quaint" bed and breakfast.

THE Cancer
Seeks Emotional Security

LEO

July 23 - Aug 22

has the Consciousness of an "Aristocrat"

Leo is the fifth sign of the zodiac, and is primarily focused on: "the inner child", the will, the ego, self expression, career, acceptance, personal love, affection, the father, men, children, entertainment and speculation.

The sign Leo represents the leader, the authority and the *"showman,"* the gregarious individual, who always takes center stage.

This *dramatic*, big-hearted fire sign, frequently exhibits the behaviors and characteristics of his zodiac symbol (the lion); having a swagger or dignified walk, possessing a large or broad upper torso, sporting a full crop of light color hair and being extremely playful. The Leo is a fun person, who loves life, and has a zest for living, enjoys performing and socializing, takes delight in parties, parades and the circus, is very fond of: games, especially games of chance, also toys, pets, "rich foods", the color yellow, cosmetics, flamboyant clothing and ornate gold jewelry.

When you are selecting a gift for a "Leo type" person, choose things that will make the individual "look and feel" like a King or Queen.

Creative • Confident Commanding

Gift Suggestions for
LEO

Give a greeting card that displays a picture of a crown or star, also use a gold ribbon when wrapping Leo's gift. Consider giving things that are associated with *royalty*: a set of goblets, gold coins, a jewelry box and a "regal looking" robe. Choose items that will enhance the Leo's appearance, performance or *creativity*: a cosmetic procedure, body care products, face, teeth and nail treatments, a day at a beauty salon or spa; also look in, or give a gift card to the game, clothing and jewelry stores. Think about giving: a trip to a creative arts or sports camp, lessons or items related to acting, singing and dancing; also consider a Toast Master course and a karaoke sound system.

Make the Leo feel like a *celebrity*; throw a BIG BASH, have a fireworks display and invite all his friends. Give: exercise or athletic equipment, an appointment with a masseur and a membership to an "exclusive" fitness center.

Shop for things related to work: the latest in computer and electronics, a gold pen and pencil set, personalized stationery and a paperweight in the shape of a lion. Purchase items, books or subscriptions about: Show Business, restaurants, recreation, romance, fashion, Hollywood, parenting, business and financial investing. Give: a captain's chair, a horoscope reading, a photo session for the Leo and his pet, lottery tickets and DVD musicals; also consider tickets to: the theater, a theme park, a sporting event, a charity affair or an evening out at a gambling casino.

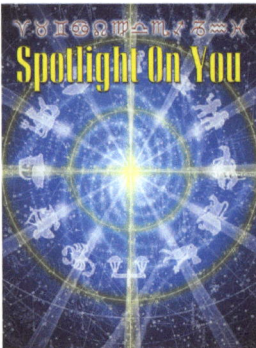

Surprise the Leo with: a romantic weekend "getaway", a bunch of colorful balloons and a BIG stuffed toy animal. Think grandiose, give: a *lavish* trip, car or boat, a home theater system and a "HUGE" hot tub or barbecue grill.

THE Leo
Seeks The Spotlight

VIRGO
Aug 23 - Sept 23

has the Consciousness of a "Good Samaritan"

Virgo is the sixth sign of the zodiac, and is primarily focused on: analyzing information, the daily habits and work routines, the maintenance of health, food preparation, the work environment and coworkers.

The sign Virgo represents the "*perfectionist*", the *discriminating* individual, who seeks to refine, purify and perfect his environment, including his body, mind and spirit. This *methodical, technical-minded* earth sign is fond of making lists, devising systems and keeping schedules, takes pleasure in reading, gardening and "puttering" around the house, favors the earth tones and the color gray, sees beauty in order, cares about animals, has an "eye" for detail, appreciates cleanliness, likes mathematics and prefers natural fibers and products.

When you are selecting a gift for a "Virgo type" person, choose things that are practical, functional and will help the individual in his daily activities; also consider things that will engage the Virgo's reasoning skills and abilities.

Dedicated • Diligent Discerning

Gift Suggestions for
VIRGO

Consider: courses of study, educational CD's and mentally challenging games. Purchase a bookstore gift card or give subscriptions, books and items related to: computers, electronics, science, cooking, carpentry, wood carving, arts and crafts, show animals, health, nutrition, landscaping, hobbies and "Do It Yourself Projects."

The Virgo has a natural curiosity about "how things work." Consider a microscope or a chemistry set, also trips to a vineyard, a dairy farm or a candy factory. Choose items associated with work or education: a desk set or a notebook computer, also a tool case, a stainless steel thermos and work attire.

The Virgo is very *precise*, give digital items: a watch, a radio, a camera, an outdoor thermometer or a bathroom scale. Look for items that will keep things in order: a closet storage system, a sewing basket, a recipe organizer and a daily planner book. Browse through the culinary shop, garden center, stationery or hardware store. Shop for: a dental care system, a First Aid kit, grooming aids and health devices, also an air or water purifier, an organic fruit basket, a juicer, an herb garden and a gift certificate to a vitamin store. Give exercise or sports equipment, athletic wear and sessions with a personal trainer. Consider giving a trip to a religious site, a stay at a beach cottage or health resort. The Virgo appreciates the "simple things in life", give a "home-cooked" meal, cleaning equipment (a power washer, a sanitary steamer, etc.); also consider giving tickets for: a ball game, a science museum, a crafts show, a concert or a movie.

THE Virgo
has a Need to Give Service

LIBRA
Sept 23 - Oct 23

has the Consciousness of a "Counselor"

Libra is the seventh sign of the zodiac, and is primarily focused on: public relations, social interaction, artistic design, fairness and equality, conflict resolution, negotiations, significant relationships, marriage, business partnerships and competitors.

The sign Libra represents the *"peace maker;"* the *diplomatic* individual, who seeks balance and harmony in life. This *poised*, very *pleasant* air sign enjoys traveling, *socializing* and *companionship*, possesses an "eye" for color and design, favors the pastel colors, especially the color green, has sophisticated tastes, and is enamored with "High Fashion", stylish hair do's and *gracious* living.

When you are selecting a gift for a "Libra type" person, choose things of beauty, refinement and culture; also consider things that will reflect the individual's mental abilities and interests.

Charming • Captivating Cooperative

Gift Suggestions for
LIBRA

The Libra takes a great interest in his physical appearance, consider giving: a full length mirror, a vanity set, a clothing valet, make-up accessories and personal grooming aids, also a gift card for: a hair procedure, a face, teeth and nail treatments, cosmetic surgery, an appointment with a fashion consultant and a day at a hair salon or spa. Give: attractive active wear, also a membership to a health club and classes for yoga, tennis or dancing. Purchase items, DVD's, books and magazine subscriptions related to: romance, relationships, the Arts, social etiquette, diet, beauty and fashion, decorating, architecture, floral arranging, graphic arts and the legal system.

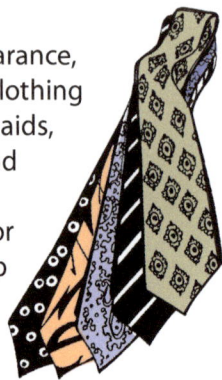

Browse in the computer, electronics and photography stores. Consider giving a dinner at an elegant restaurant, also give tickets to: a sporting or social event, a concert, a fashion show, an art exhibit or a theatrical production. Purchase: a silk scarf or tie, custom-made apparel, a pair of soft and supple gloves, a hand bag and a hair ornament.

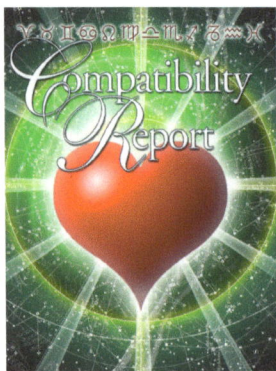

Think about: a tandem bicycle, a gift card for a car wash & wax, art supplies, mentally stimulating games, travel accessories, a wireless phone, a wine rack, modeling classes and an astrological compatibility reading. Consider engaging a house cleaning, landscaping or decorating service. Give the Libra things that are *tasteful* and thoughtful; such as: a single rose, an intimate picnic, a romantic CD or an original poem. Also give things that are monogrammed: towels, jewelry, clothing, or stationery. The Libra has an appreciation for the "finer things" of life; give: designer clothes, jewelry and fragrances, also fine furs, wines, linens and art, luxury cars, cruises and trips.

THE Libra
Seeks A Partner

SCORPIO
Oct 23 - Nov 22

has the Consciousness of a "Researcher"

Scorpio is the eighth sign of the zodiac, and is primarily focused on: strong emotions, work, resource development, anything that is owned jointly, the cycle of death and rebirth, health, transformation, healing, reinvention and the occult, also trust, control, sex, secrets and letting-go. The sign Scorpio represents the "*investigator*", the probing individual, who delves into the deep *mysteries* of life. This *highly intuitive, emotionally intense* water sign is always prepared, and knows the answer before he asks the question, is fascinated with magic, the metaphysical, forensic science, the supernatural and the medieval period, enjoys music, puzzles, *detective* stories and *psychological* thrillers, is comfortable working with machinery, hardware and sharp instruments, favors the colors black, wine and burgundy, and is fond of: leather, cosmetics, jewelry, body piercing and "the night life".

When selecting a gift for a Scorpio type person, choose an item that will stir the passions.

Powerful • Persistent Persuasive

Gift Suggestions for
SCORPIO

Give: a membership to a health club, classes for boxing, fencing or Martial Arts, exercise equipment and sessions with a personal trainer; also consider: cosmetic surgery, personal fragrances and grooming aids, a teeth whitening treatment and a gift card for a facial or deep body massage. Look in: the computer, stationery and electronics stores, also the auto, clothing and tattoo shops. Purchase subscriptions, books or items related to: science, *psychology*, *self-development*, motorcycles, archaeology, mechanics, Egyptian culture, astrology, herpetology, the stock market and gemology. Think about turning Scorpio's spare room into his very own *private* sanctuary. Browse in the religious or the metaphysical stores. Give yoga lessons, aroma therapies or a personal horoscope reading. Purchase items for the Scorpio's bedroom, bathroom or work; such as: satin sheets, bedroom apparel, a shower massager, precision tools and all types of organizers. Think about: a dragon game, music CD or CD player, a "head to toe" make-over, dance or music lessons, health devices, a paper shredder, a security system, power tools, a metal sculpture, a cutlery set and a motor vehicle. Put the Scorpio, in or near, his element: an indoor waterfall, a dinner cruise, scuba diving lessons, and a deep-sea fishing trip. Think about giving tickets to: a musical, a murder mystery weekend and shows featuring a magician or hypnotist.

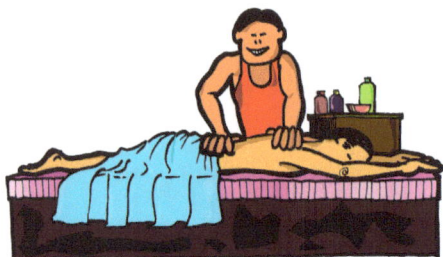

Give things that will increase the Scorpio's "net worth"; such as: a monthly financial newsletter, cash, stocks, real estate, fine art and antiques, also precious stones, metals and gold coins.

THE Scorpio
Seeks Emotional Intimacy

SAGITTARIUS
Nov 22 - Dec 21

has the Consciousness of a "World Traveler/Educator"

Sagittarius is the ninth sign of the zodiac, and is primarily focused on: a deeper meaning and understanding of life, higher education, long distance communication and travel, mass media, commerce, shipping, imports-exports, foreign affairs (people, places and things), also the judicial system, principles, ethics, religious beliefs and cultural attitudes.

The sign Sagittarius represents a *"free spirit"*; the *adventurous* individual, who wants to *experience* life to its fullest, and is willing to take the *risks*, to do it. This *outgoing, optimistic* fire sign is a combination of both, the mental and physical energies; loves language, learning and philosophical discourse, enjoys sports and "the great outdoors", appreciates and respects the laws of nature, likes things done on a *grand scale*, prefers loose-fitting clothing, favors the color purple, and is fond of *large* animals, especially horses.

When you are selecting a gift for a "Sagittarius type" person, choose things that will excite and challenge the body, mind and spirit.

Positive • Principled Prosperous

Gift Suggestions for
SAGITTARIUS

Consider giving things that will *expand* the Sagittarian's consciousness: a short wave radio, a trip to a foreign country, travel DVD's, a visit to a national park or zoo, a world globe or a dinner at an ethnic restaurant, also a membership to a book club, a PC, a big screen TV, educational courses, CD's and games, a horoscope reading and tickets to a lecture or museum. Purchase books and magazine subscriptions for: travel, wildlife, log homes, geography, world events, the law, politics, philosophy, the internet, astrology or a foreign language, and also classes or items related to wine tasting, international cooking, archery, flying, skiing, horseback riding and wilderness survival. Visit the religious and metaphysical shops.

Consider turning the Sagittarian's spare room into a library; one with plenty of bookshelves, for all those trophies, sports memorabilia and literary classics. Give items that have a cultural motif; such as Mexican pottery or African art. Browse in the Wilderness store; look at: camping, kayaking, hunting and fishing gear.

The Sagittarius is always "on the go"; look at items related to travel and mobility: a horse, a car or a boat, a mountain bike, a GPS and a membership to an auto club, also luggage, a passbook case, a wireless phone, a PDA and a portable TV.

Think about giving: tickets for a horse or air show, a ship's cruise and a jungle safari, also a stay at a dude ranch, a mountain lodge or a religious site.

THE Sagittarius
Needs Freedom

CAPRICORN
Dec 22 -Jan 19

has the Consciousness of an "Authority Figure"

Capricorn is the tenth sign of the zodiac, and is primarily focused on: work, career, the corporate world, government, duty, reputation, social position and responsibility, honors, recognition and success in the outer world. The sign Capricorn represents the *"achiever,"* the *ambitious* individual, who sets *goals*, is *self - disciplined* and strives for *excellence*.

This *conventional*, *serious-minded* earth sign has strong ties to family, home and country, is fond of tradition, history, politics and things from the past, wears the colors dark blue and black, appreciates formality, organization and structure, has a good work ethic and is enamored with status symbols.

When you are selecting a gift for a "Capricorn type" person, think in terms of superlatives; "the finest and the very best".

Realistic • Responsible Respectable

Gift Suggestions for
CAPRICORN

Give items that create an "*air of professionalism*", such as: new office equipment or furniture, a set of hand-crafted tools, a leather attache and a personalized business card case.

Consider: educational courses, CD's and games, especially games dealing with history, career and real estate. Purchase books, magazine subscriptions or items pertaining to: antiques, home beautification, fine dining, castles, classic cars, social etiquette, financial investing and strategies for business success; also consider a gift card to a bookstore that carries "first editions" and leather bound books.

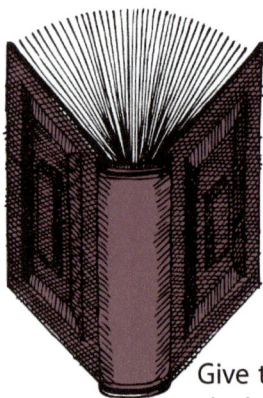

Think about engaging a genealogist or photographer to do a family tree, crest or photo. Shop for: ski equipment, climbing gear, coffee table books, religious or patriotic items, classical music CD's or a trip to an historical site. Look for products that will enhance the appearance of the hair, skin or teeth.

Choose items that will keep things in order: a trophy cabinet, a CD case, a desk organizer and custom-made bookshelves.

Give the Capricorn: a family heirloom, a grandfather clock, an "old time" radio, a juke box and some vintage movie DVD's. Choose things that will keep the Capricorn "nice and warm": a handsome hat, coat or afghan.

Consider: tickets to the theater, an Ice show, an opera, a concert, or a black tie affair. Give *prestigious* items: an expensive time piece, fine art, wine, china and linens, designer clothes or jewelry, dinner at a gourmet restaurant and box seats to a sporting event, also a luxury trip, car or cruise.

THE Capricorn
has a Need to Accomplish

AQUARIUS
Jan 19 - Feb 18

has the Consciousness of a"Humanitarian"

Aquarius is the eleventh sign of the zodiac, and is primarily concerned with: The universal laws, spiritual awakening, the future, group consciousness, community, impersonal love, brotherhood, clubs and organizations, friendships, "hopes and wishes", "the unexpected" and controversy, also science, advanced technology, aeronautics and the occult.

The sign Aquarius represents the "*original* thinker"; the *progressive* individual, who introduces new and *revolutionary* ideas. This highly *unconventional independent air sign* has many friends, but only one or two close confidants, is a nonconformist, thrives on anticipation, wants to share knowledge, takes delight in surprising others, is willing to try "anything", and is fond of: computers, electrical gadgets, science fiction, astrology, the plaid design and things that are *avant-garde*.

When you are selecting a gift for an "Aquarius type" person, choose things that are novel, exotic or unusual; also consider giving things that will nourish the intellectual mind.

Inventive • Innovative Ingenious

Gift Suggestions for
AQUARIUS

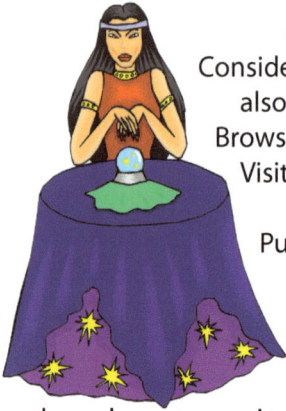

Consider giving: a horoscope, tarot or psychic reading, also zodiac jewelry, astrology books and calendars. Browse through the metaphysical or New Age shops. Visit the computer, small appliance and electronics stores for the latest in "Hi Tech" products. Purchase items, books or magazine subscriptions pertaining to: politics, social issues, advocacy groups, outer space, UFO's, astronomy scientific inventions and the Internet. Consider giving: mentally challenging games and puzzles, a course in writing, speaking or computers, a bookstore gift card, a telescope, a cactus farm, an abstract painting, classes for acting, a personalized anklet and a book of famous quotations; also consider items that use a remote control: a robot, a sound system and a garage door opener. Keep the Aquarian warm with a plaid sweater, a pair of ear muffs or an electric blanket.

The sign Aquarius is associated with *contradictions;* for instance, the individual likes to be part of the group, and yet, he wants to stand out in a crowd. Consider giving some outrageous clothing item or accessory; such as a bizarre looking chapeau, scarf or umbrella.

Check-out your mail order catalogs or novelty shops for items that are *unique* and *different.* Think about: an expedition to a cold climate, also a trip to a planetarium, a space center or a science museum. Give airline tickets, flying lessons or a ride in a hot air balloon. Consider: tickets to an *"off beat"* Broadway show, a donation to the Aquarian's favorite charity or a dinner with *friends*, at a bohemian restaurant.

THE Aquarius
Wants Change

PISCES
Feb 18 - March 20

has the Consciousness of a "Rescuer"

Pisces is the twelfth sign of the zodiac, and is primarily focused on: *feelings*, dreams, the unconscious, the unforeseen, endings and completions, spiritual reality, karma, forgiveness, faith, hope and charity, also the creative arts and the element of water.

The sign Pisces represents the *"artist/visionary"*; the *psychic* individual, who is attuned to another dimension. This gentle, "dreamy eyed" water sign is highly idealistic and imaginative, takes delight in fairy tales, fantasy and illusion, enjoys movies, music, television and photography, is sensitive to subtle odors and fragrances, and is very fond of sea creatures, small animals and the ocean.

When you are selecting a gift for a "Pisces type" person, choose items that will connect with the *"inner spirit"*.

Sweet • Sensitive Selfless

Gift Suggestions for
PISCES

Choose items that are mystical, unusual or have an ethereal quality; such as: a miniature indoor tranquility pond, a horoscope, tarot or psychic reading, yoga lessons, a harp instrument or music CD, scented candles and aroma therapies, also beautiful flowers or art, delicate jewelry, a book of poetry and a romantic music CD.

Give tickets to an art exhibit, a symphony concert or the ballet. Look in the religious or metaphysical shops; consider: crystals, runes, meditation CD's or religious items. Give things that will help the Piscean in his *artistic* endeavors: acting, painting and sculpting lessons, art supplies, a writing course, a PC and a gift card to the book or stationery stores.

Shop for things that are related to water: a sailboat, a CD featuring "the sounds of the seashore", fishing or scuba diving gear, also beach, boating and water sports equipment. Give an aquatic garden, a swimming pool, a hot tub, a shower CD player, a gift card to the tropical fish store, a seafood dinner and items that have a nautical theme; also consider tickets to the aquarium, a Water Park or Ice Show. Purchase items associated with the feet; give a gift card to a shoe store, a pair of ice skates, a pedicure, a foot massage, dance lessons or a "night out dancing". Look for items associated with the bedroom: a new mattress, an air room purifier, a clock radio, bedroom linens and apparel.

The Piscean, from time to time, has a need to withdraw from the "outer world"; think about giving: movie tickets, a sound system with headphones, a ship's cruise, a religious retreat and a stay at a *secluded* seaside cottage.

THE Pisces
Wants To Be Helpful

About the Author

Carol Sandy, of Clark, New Jersey, has been an astrologer for 30 years. She has an astrological business offered primarily through her website, **Astro Window**, *http://www.astrowindow.com*.

Carol makes a special point, in her business, of reaching out to people who are new to astrology, and offering them introductory materials. For example, she has self-published other introductory books, such as *The Sun Sign Life Guide*. This fourteen page guide is given to each of her clients as a free extra with a Natal Horoscope reading. It has information about Sun signs, but also introduces the Solar Return chart and its preparation. Carol's thrust is to encourage her readers and clients to become more centered and connected to the higher self. She specializes in natal and compatibility readings.

Carol also is an active blogger, and uses this medium to teach astrology through her "Welcome to the Astro Window Classroom." . See her articles and lessons with assignments in the archives. You'll find links on her website, or just go to:

http://astrologyandgifts.blogspot.com

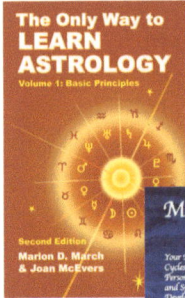
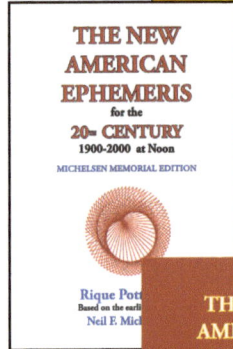
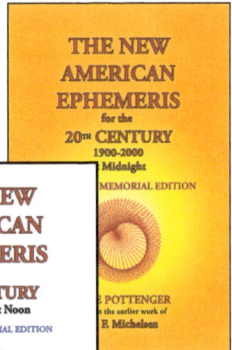
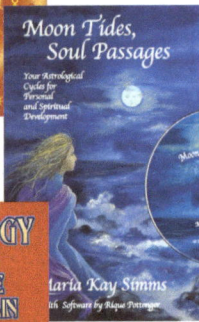
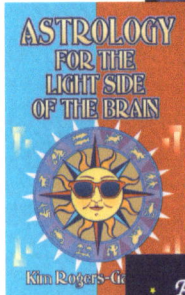
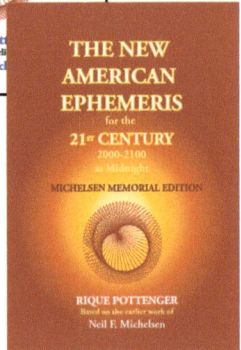
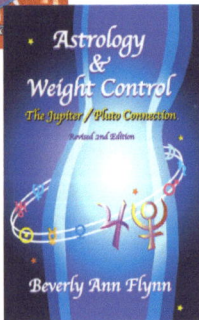

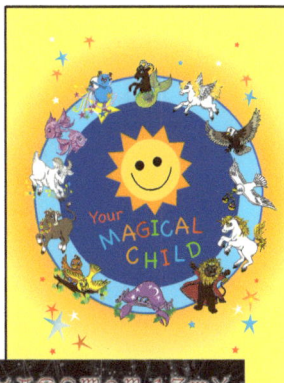

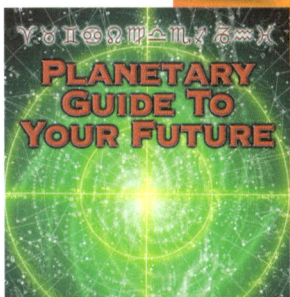

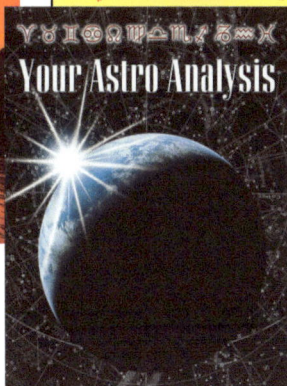

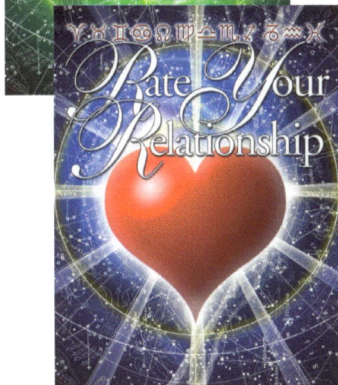

Your Horoscope

**View your life from a different perspective
with an audio natal horoscope reading from the
author of this book, Carol Sandy!**

Although Sun sign astrology is valid; it is incomplete, since it only deals with one facet of an individual's personality or energy pattern, his Sun sign. Each individual is uniquely different, and so too, is his natal horoscope. The only true way of obtaining a comprehensive picture of an individual and his life experiences, is with a natal horoscope; a map of the heavens at a specific time, date and place (a nativity).

The premise in metaphysical astrology is that *the heavens mirror the earth*; therefore by being aware of the planetary activities, the astrologer has insight into the past, understands the present and can predict the future.

The natal horoscope represents an individual's potential for personal and spiritual growth; however, it is always up the individual (his will, determination and intelligence), how he chooses to use his energies. The natal horoscope offers the individual insight into his attitudes, behaviors, inner conflicts, challenges, lessons, needs, talents, opportunities, and most importantly, the individual's life purpose.

Visit Carol's website for more details

Astro Window
http://www.astrowindow.com

Email: *astrowindow@aol.com*
Phone: 732-382-0105
PO Box 5813
Clark, NJ 07066-2424

*Natal horoscope readings are provided on audio CD.
All readings are made personally and specifically
for each individual client.*